SKETCHING

℞

RAVETTE PUBLISHING

Printed and bound for Ravette Publishing Limited
Unit 3, Tristar Centre, Star Road,
Partridge Green, West Sussex RH13 8RA
by STIGE, Italy.
Photography by Peter Raymond, Southport.
Origination by DL Repro Ltd., London EC1M 4DD.
Typeset by John O'Hanlon, Southport.
ISBN 1 85304 829 1

Winsor and Newton brushes, paints and artists'
materials together with Conté sketching and pastel
materials are used throughout this book and are
recommended by artist Philip Berrill.

CONTENTS

EVERYONE'S GUIDE TO SKETCHING CONTAINS 27 DEMONSTRATIONS FOR YOU TO TRY.

Philip Berrill "The Flying Artist"

Philip Berrill was born in 1945 in Northampton. Philip is a professional artist, art tutor, lecturer and author whose techniques and methods of learning to paint are taught and enjoyed worldwide. Philip now lives in Southport with his wife Sylvia. They have a daughter Penelope. Philip first recalls discovering paint at the age of three. It was one sunny summer afternoon. Philip wandered into his father's glasshouse. At the end of the glasshouse stood a large bucket of whitewash and a tubular pump type sprayer. Philip loaded it with whitewash from the bucket and had a lovely afternoon spraying all his father's best tomatoes and plants white. The entire inside of the glasshouse was covered with whitewash. Philip had discovered paint, and that with paint you could change the world. His father returned to find his glasshouse a white house and his son dripping from head to foot with whitewash, a white paint.

At the age of 14 Philip decided he wanted to make a living as a professional artist, having always enjoyed art at school where he came under the influence, and studied under, the Welsh artist and tutor, John Sullivan. Philip's love and enthusiasm for sketching and painting is infectious. He believes that art should be for everyone and he continues to enjoy passing on his enthusiasm and knowledge of how to sketch and paint, gained over 30 years, to people of all ages. His art courses, TV art series and "Painting for Pleasure" Roadshows have always proved popular and in great demand worldwide.

Philip held his first one-man exhibition at the age of 18. Other group and one-man exhibitions followed. At the age of 28 a major exhibition of his work was held at Liverpool University. The exhibition was opened by the renowned BBC radio and TV broadcaster Brian Redhead. As a direct result of this exhibition Philip realised his ambition to become established as a professional artist and launched his very successful art classes using his own special approach to teaching sketching and painting. These proved so popular the artist developed his worldwide correspondence art courses. In the 1980s painting holiday courses in Great Britain followed and these led to organising and tutoring on painting holiday courses in Europe, in Rome, Venice, Florence and Paris. Philip was invited to lecture and demonstrate painting on sea cruises. Demonstration and lecture visits followed to Houston, Dallas and Dubai. Philip's exhibition "The Italian Connection", an exhibition of his sketches and paintings of his Italian journeys and other European locations, was very well received.

Philip enjoys and is experienced in painting everything from miniatures to murals. His paintings and signed limited edition prints are owned by patrons worldwide. His murals are found in private and public locations.

Philip Berrill with actor/comedian Norman Wisdom who appears in Philip's televison art series.

Philip, whose sketching and painting courses and techniques are designed to be suitable for people of all abilities and all ages, found great enjoyment in the challenge of producing his own art videos. These led to the invitation to produce and present his own 13 part television series, "Paint with the Flying Artist", and now to the invitation to write and illustrate his own series of art books specially for you. The books "Everyone's Guide to..." are designed to cover a wide range of mediums, techniques and subjects to introduce you to the joy and pleasure of sketching and painting.

You are never too young or too old to start sketching. Philip's students have ranged from 10 to 80 years of age. They come from all walks of life; school children, housewives, doctors, nurses, shop workers, industrial workers, managers, accountants, farm workers, bankers and people who have retired, almost every background imaginable. Everyone can enjoy the art of sketching and painting.

Below. Philip was painting one day in Venice. A film crew appeared and started to record a television commercial close by. The model, the car and the wonderful Venetian backdrop presented a new subject. Philip broke off from the scene he was painting and using pen and wash quickly sketched this unique subject.

Above. Students of all ages watch a demonstration by Philip Berrill

Introduction

"A B S" Always Be Sketching, is a favourite saying of mine. If you have ever said "I wish I could paint, but I can't draw a straight line", then sketching could be the first step to introducing you to the marvellous world of art. Sketching can be fun in its own right, and is also quite simply the key to creating successful paintings. It is the most economical introduction to learning the essentials of picture making. Experience has taught me that many people who already paint greatly underestimate the value of sketching. No matter whether you are a newcomer to painting, or you are at a more advanced stage, I invite you to join with me to read and sketch your way through this book, "Everyone's Guide to Sketching", to discover the delights sketching can offer you.

Most of the great masters were great sketchers. If they found sketching important and worthwhile, we should take sketching equally seriously. What is a sketch? It is important to spend a few moments thinking and analysing exactly what a sketch is. What does it set out to achieve? How much information is included in a sketch? Can you sketch in different mediums? Is a sketch just made in black and white or can you sketch in colour? What is the difference between a sketch and a drawing?

A sketch is a versatile way to express ideas and to put down on paper the initial visual information about a subject. The subject can be real, from a photograph, inspired by poetry, prose or music, or from your imagination. The sketch is often the first exploratory stage for a painting. It can be part of the preparation, which may include one or more sketches, to explore, play with and develop an idea or subject into a foundation for a finished drawing or painting. Sketches should be flexible in that they can be altered, changed and adapted. Sometimes a sketch is just a few fleeting lines that capture the essentials of the subject. At other times a sketch may contain more information, including details on light and shade, textures and colour notes. When you do not have time to paint a picture of an eye-catching view you can make a quick sketch and take a photograph of it. The sketch and photograph will allow you to paint a picture of the view at home or in your studio.

Anything that makes a mark can be used to sketch with. The great joy of sketching is that you can start with a humble pencil on the back of an envelope. Many sketches have a spontaneity and freshness that at first people find difficult to capture in a finished painting. This is often because one is more relaxed when sketching and less worried about making mistakes. At first when painting, people try too hard to get the painting just right. The spontaneity in a painting comes from speed, the speed from experience and the experience from practice. Sketching is a wonderful form of practice. A sketch can contain as little or as much information as you feel necessary. In a drawing, the subject, content, composition and style have been decided on by the artist. A sketch tends to be looser, more exploratory and sometimes seems a little incomplete. However, many a sketch will stand as an attractive, keepable, frameable and saleable work of art in its own right. Sketching is essentially the visual expression of ideas about real or imaginary subjects. Let your sketching be fun.

Top right. Students enjoying an outdoor demonstration.

Right. Activity painting holidays are very popular. After a day's sketching, members of Philip's Mediterranean holiday painting cruise relax in the ship's lounge.

Below. A selection of sketches from Philip's portfolio.

Materials for Sketching

Almost anything that can make a mark can be used to sketch with. I am sure many parents have watched the expression of sheer enjoyment on the face of a child when he or she finds and picks up a pencil, crayon or pen and starts to scribble and make marks with it. The child has discovered something that he or she can play and express themselves with. Sometimes parents have found to their horror that children enjoy their new found form of expression by drawing on walls of the family home. Do encourage children to sketch and paint at the earliest possible age. Let them have lots of paper, pencils and crayons to play with. We so easily forget that once upon a time all the great masters, including Leonardo da Vinci, Michelangelo, Raphael, Renoir and Van Gogh were children. Who is to say that a great master of tomorrow is not a child in your own town, your own street or even in your own home today?

The early cave painters of France and Spain produced the most dramatic of images with very basic materials which they found around them in their own environment. There was no prehistoric art shop along the road in which to buy art materials. They had to improvise in the creation of their own sketching and painting materials. There were no art teachers to help them, yet they produced stunning pictures based on their own life and experiences as a means of communicating their images and thoughts to their fellow cave dwellers. We are fortunate. We have a superb selection of art materials conveniently available from art shops at affordable prices. The materials we buy and use today have been made based on the knowledge, skills, experience and needs of artists, and from their desire to create images over the centuries.

All you need to start sketching is a pencil and a sheet of paper. If you look round your home, you may be amazed at the many other suitable materials you will find to hand, including ballpoint pens, pencils, fountain pens, felt-tipped and nylon-tipped pens, coloured pens and plain typing or writing paper. It is possible to sketch in a wide range of other mediums including coloured pencils, water colours, pastels and oil paints. We will look at these techniques in later stages in this book.

Let us now look at the extensive range of materials available for sketching. I will then list what I call "The Essential Sketching Kit" which will tell you the items you will need.

PENCILS

Conté are amongst the leaders in the manufacture of pencils and sketching materials for artists. Pencils are made from a mixture of graphite and china clay. The more graphite there is in the pencil the softer it is, and the darker the mark it will make. The more china clay in the mixture the harder the pencil, and the sharper, less dark the line, or mark, it will make. The pencil lead is normally mounted in wood. The pencil is circular or hexagonal in shape. Soft pencils are known as B, harder pencils as H. They are also numbered 2,3,4,5,6,7,8 and 9. The higher the number, the softer, or harder, the pencil. 2B and 3B are medium soft and are ideal for sketching. 7,8 and 9 B are too soft and smudgy for general work, but do have their uses. The H pencils are too hard for most art work, being preferred for technical or engineering drawing. HB pencils are in everyday use for writing as they are an all purpose pencil, specially suitable for writing and note taking.

CARPENTERS' PENCILS

These are made in a similar manner to the traditional round pencils but are rectangular in shape. They can be sharpened to a chisel-like end and offer a different variety of pencil marks compared to the normal pencil.

GRAPHITE STICKS

These are sticks of graphite, not bound in a wooden casing but varnished or wrapped in paper to stop the graphite soiling your fingers. The main advantage is that you can use the tip as a normal pencil, but the wide side of the sharpened end can be used for bold sweeps of pencil marks and for the shading of large areas. Both carpenters' pencils and graphite sticks can be obtained in varying B degrees of softness.

PENS

Dip-in, sketching or mapping pens are the most common. These have a metallic nib in a wooden or plastic holder. The pen is dipped into ink to load the nib of the pen.

INDIAN AND COLOURED INKS

Indian ink is black and lightfast. It is obtainable in waterproof and non-waterproof forms. I recommend the waterproof version for sketching. Coloured inks are also available. The main problem with them is that when exposed to normal daylight for any length of time the coloured inks are, in many instances, fugitive and can fade. They are ideally suited to work that will not be exposed to a great deal of light.

FOUNTAIN PENS

The regular fountain pen can be used to sketch with. Some manufacturers have a range of sketching pens, like fountain pens, on the market. These use non-waterproof ink in cartridges. Do not use Indian ink with these, or with fountain pens. Indian ink contains a mild glue and can clog a fountain pen. Use regular fountain pen ink. Use Indian ink for dip-in pens or brush drawing work.

BALLPOINT PENS

The domestic ballpoint pen is an ideal tool for quick sketching.

FELT-TIP AND NYLON-TIP PENS

The tremendous number, range of sizes and types of points on modern felt and synthetic-tip pens provide a bewildering choice for the artist. Experiment; find one or two pens you feel comfortable with. Some pens are waterproof, others are not. Most of the coloured pens will fade in strong light. Ask your local art or stationery store to explain the qualities of the various pens they stock. Many have sample pens you can try out in the store.

COLOURED PENCILS

Some coloured pencils are water soluble, often known as aquarelle, others are not water soluble and are used just for applying dry colour. Conté Aquarelle pencils can be used dry, or brushed over with a wash of water to create water colour-like effects. A set of Aquarelle pencils provides a variety of ways of using colour in sketches.

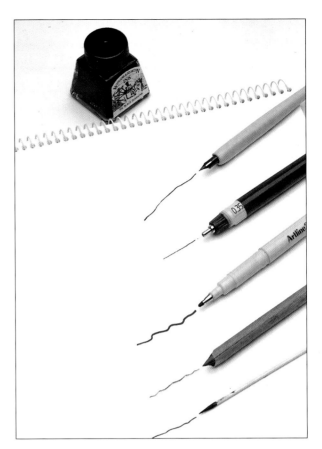

CONTÉ CARRES: CRAYONS

These are square sticks of firm pastel. The most common colours are black, grey, white, sanguine and sepia. They offer delightful results, specially on tinted paper.

SEPIA, SANGUINE AND WHITE CONTÉ PASTEL PENCILS

These also offer exciting sketching opportunities when working on tinted paper.

CONTÉ CARBON GRAPHIC PENCIL

This is designed for finer, more defined lines and is ideal for sketching and technical drawing.

CONTÉ PIERRE NOIRE

This is made from a filtered paste pigment and gives deep, solid and indelible matt blacks every time.

CHARCOAL

Black, burnt wood. This is usually made from willow wood and is available in single sticks or boxed in thin, medium, thick or assorted sticks. Charcoal can be reduced to powder by the manufacturers, remixed and reformed into compressed sticks of charcoal in different pencil like degrees of softness.

ERASERS

The India eraser is the general all-purpose eraser, but the one preferred by most artists is the putty eraser, so called because it can be moulded with the fingers into all manner of practical shapes for rubbing out, modifying and lifting out passages of work. Also, it does not create lots of loose pieces of paper and eraser so the work does not have to be dusted off with the hand. This reduces the risk of smudging.

FIXATIVE

Pencils, charcoal and Conté pastels need "fixing" to prevent them smudging. Clear fixative is widely available in aerosol can form, but can also be obtained in a bottle with a mouthpiece diffuser for use in the traditional manner. The aerosol can is far more convenient.

PAPER

Cartridge paper is the most popular for sketching and can be obtained by the sheet or in pad, spiral bound and gummed book forms. "A" sizes are commonly used. A1 = 594mm x 841mm, A2 = 420mm x 594mm, A3 = 297mm x 420mm, A4 = 210mm x 297mm, A5 = 148mm x 210mm, and A6 = 105mm x 148mm. Different sizes can be used for different subjects and for different occasions. Cartridge paper can be obtained in different weights and thicknesses but 110gram paper is ideal for most sketching work.

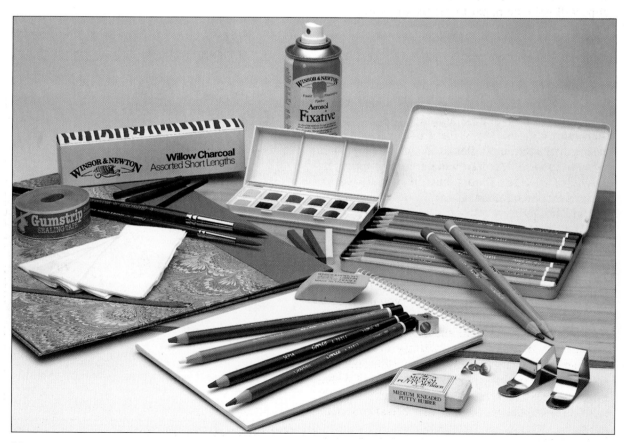

BRUSHES

Round and flat, sable, or the modern synthetic hair brushes enable colour to be used either directly, or in conjunction with another sketching medium. The Winsor and Newton Cotman and Sceptre ranges are specially good value for money.

PENCIL SHARPENERS, CRAFT KNIVES AND GLASSPAPER

Bring the pencil point to the shape you would like to use for the sketch you plan to make using a pencil sharpener, craft knife and glasspaper.

PAINTS

A Winsor and Newton pocket set of Artist Qualtity, or Cotman, water colour 1/2 pans will provide a compact set of paints for indoor and outdoor sketching.

DRAWING BOARDS

Some people prefer to work on a sketch pad with its rigid back as the support for their paper. If using a drawing board, an A2 or A3 size is practical for indoor use but too heavy for outdoor use. A sheet of smooth, brown hardboard is lighter and handier for outdoor use.

DRAWING PINS, DRAWING BOARD CLIPS, MASKING TAPE

Try not to use drawing pins as they make marks in the board which can show through in other work if shading or drawing over the holes. Drawing board clips will hold the paper to the board, but I usually secure my paper to the board with masking tape.

TISSUES

Soft tisuues are handy for wiping your pen nib or brush when sketching or painting.

EASEL

An easel is not essential for sketching. However, table easels are available and many people enjoy working on them. The Winsor and Newton table easel adjusts to four angles of incline and folds flat when not in use. Metal or wooden sketching easels can be very useful indoors, but are specially useful on outdoor sketching trips.

PORTFOLIO

An A3 or A4 portfolio will keep your sketches clean and flat.

THE ESSENTIAL SKETCHING KIT.
I recommend that you collect together the following essential items as they will enable you to enjoy a wide range of sketching techniques. An A4 or A3 cartridge sketch pad, a 2B and a 3B pencil, a pencil sharpener or craft knife, a putty eraser, fine glasspaper, a mapping pen, a bottle of Indian ink, a fine nylon or felt-tip pen, a pocket set of water colours, a No. 6 round water colour brush, a half inch (13mm) flat wash brush, tissues and two small pots for water.

Table easel

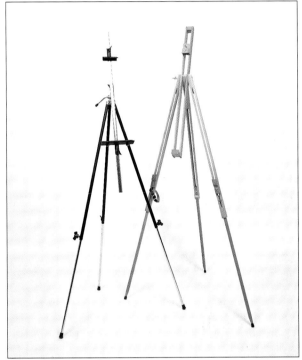

Sketching easels

The essential sketching kit

11

Sketching: How To Get Started

There are almost as many styles of sketching as there are artists. Everyone's style of handwriting differs and so do styles of sketching. My own style is neat and tidy, but I have seen and equally enjoyed looking at very vigorous free flowing work by other artists. Look at pictures in art galleries, art publications and magazines, look at fine art prints in art shops and stores to discover the very many and varied styles artists have used and continue to use. One artist may use a few quick lines to encapsulate the subject, another may use many lines. One artist may use little or no colour, another could use vibrant colours in his or her interpretation of the same subject. You may be attracted by the style of one artist and not another, but think how boring it would be if all sketches and paintings looked the same. Explore your own natural style by trying subjects in different sketching mediums.

With the tree I used a 2B pencil for the pencil sketch, then I tried a monchrome sketch using a water soluble felt-tip pen and created a monochrome by brushing over it with a little water. Finally, I made a pen and wash sketch in colour.

Pencil

A water soluble felt-tip pen brushed with water

Pen and Wash

Demonstration 1
Let's Get To The Point

The shape of the point of your pencil can make its own distinctive contribution to your sketch. Whilst you can just pick up a pencil and sketch away, let us think about the pencil point. Do you want a sharp point giving a fine, sharp line or a more rounded point giving a different width of line? Would a less sharp point be of benefit to a particular sketch? The way you sharpen your pencil can make quite a difference to a sketch.

Pencil sharpener and pencil

A pencil sharpener can be used to give a clear, sharp point to the pencil. But, by using a craft knife or penknife, you can vary the length of pencil lead exposed. Use the knife to slice away the wood around the pencil point. Do not try to shape the pencil lead with the knife. Always keep fingers behind cutting edges.

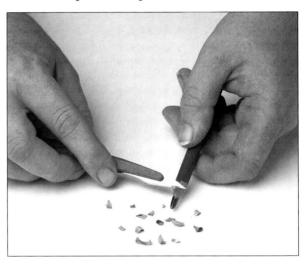

Sharpening with a knife

By rubbing the pencil point on a sheet of fine glasspaper you can make the tip more rounded, or create a chisel-like edge to the pencil tip. Try creating sharp pointed, rounded and chisel ends to your pencil and compare the types of lines created.

Using glasspaper to shape the pencil point

Demonstration 2
Sketching: Holding Your Pencil, Pen or Brush

Fingers

When first holding a pencil for drawing most people adopt the writing position. They rest their hand on the paper and hold the pencil in their fingers. This gives a small controlled area and allows for sketch lines and curves of a short length. This is fine for writing but is not practical for sketching and painting.

By lifting the hand off the page you can work from your wrist as well as your fingers. A single line, or curve, drawn from the wrist can be two to three times longer than a line drawn from the fingers when the hand is resting on the table.

Sit back in your chair with your hand still off the page. Try drawing a line from your elbow joint. This will give you considerable freedom when wanting longer, free flowing lines. You will have a much larger area for your hand and arm to sweep curved and straight lines.

Finally, with your sketch pad on an easel or a table top, stand up and draw a line from your shoulder joint. This will give you the largest possible area for your arm and hand to sweep and work within.

Try sketching lines on your sketch pad in the ways described above , working from your fingers, wrist, elbow and shoulder.

Wrist

Elbow

Shoulder

Demonstration 3
Basic Shapes

By taking things step by step and building on sound foundations you will soon find that you can begin to sketch successfully. Rather than sketching your subject from the top and working downwards, I recommend a slightly different approach. Everything you ever draw or paint will be based on one or more basic shapes; circles, ovals, squares, rectangles, triangles and cylinders. For an apple, lightly draw a simple circle. The distinctive apple shape can be sketched over that. For a coffee mug, draw a light vertical cylinder and sketch your mug on that. A combination of basic shapes makes the sketching of a traditional telephone quite an easy task. Draw a simple triangle, add a circle for a dial, two ovals and a curve for the handset and a long rectangle for the base.

Lightly drawing the basic shape, or shapes, of your subject will ensure it is going to sit in the right place on your sketch pad, and be of the right proportions. The subject should sit neither too high nor too low on the page, nor be too wide, too thin, too tall or too short.

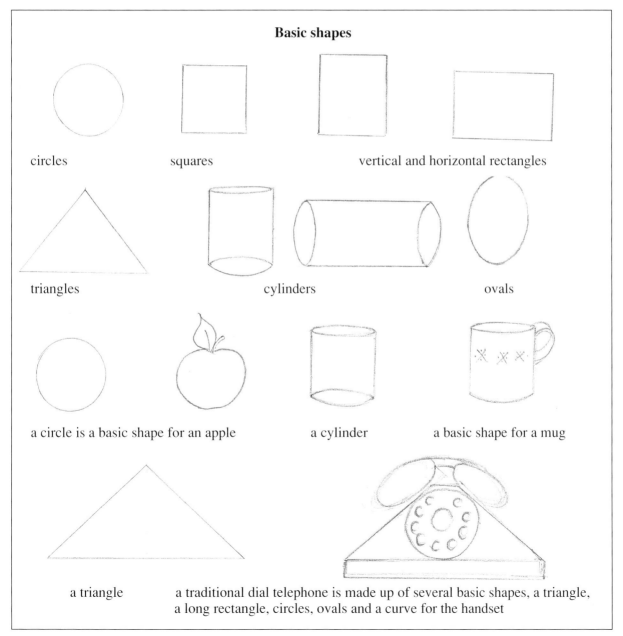

Basic shapes

circles   squares   vertical and horizontal rectangles

triangles   cylinders   ovals

a circle is a basic shape for an apple   a cylinder   a basic shape for a mug

a triangle   a traditional dial telephone is made up of several basic shapes, a triangle, a long rectangle, circles, ovals and a curve for the handset

Look around your home for objects based on basic shapes.
Circles, squares, rectangles, cylinders, ovals and triangles.
Sketch the basic shapes and then build the objects on them.

cylinder

saucepan

circle

tea pot

triangle

table lamp

square

kitchen scales

Demonstration 4
Pencil Shading

Pencils vary in degree of softness (B) and hardness (H). Copy the chart on the right into your sketch book. H pencils to the left and B pencils to the right. Look for pencils around your home, office, factory or classroom. A number and letter is usually found on the pencil end, e.g. 2B. Go to No. 2 under letter B on the chart and shade a dark to light column down the page. Vary the strength of shading by varying the pressure of your hand on the pencil. As you steadily add different degrees of pencil to your chart you will see and feel the difference in their effects.

Use a 2B pencil to make out the tone chart shown below, left. Look for, and show, three tones of shading in your subjects: light, medium and dark. Towards the end of a study always look for, and emphasise, the very darkest and the very lightest features. Soft pencil shading can be gently blended, rubbed with a fingertip, for softer shading effects.

In the bottom right panel I show how highlights can be "lifted out" with a putty eraser avoiding ragged-edged highlights.

Pencil strength chart

Pencil tonal strengths and blending technique

Lifting out highlights with a putty eraser

Demonstration 5
Shading: Points To Remember

The sketches on this page are worth copying into your sketch book as they will help you remember the important aspects of shading.

The jug. Right. Always ask yourself, and decide, which way the source of light is coming from, the left, the right or from above. Here it is coming from the left. In this sketch I have used my 2B pencil and show all three tones of shading: light, medium and dark. I then emphasised the very darkest features and picked out the highlights.

Below right. Look for, and show, the two parts to the shadows cast by objects. The shadow is darker at the base of the object and becomes lighter as it travels away.

Below left. The higher the source of light, the shorter the shadow; the lower the source of light, the longer the shadow. The stronger the light, the darker the shadow; the softer the light, the gentler the shadow.

Jug

The **higher** the source of light the shorter the shadow.

Light from **above,**

Always decide where the light source is coming from to light your subject, above, the left, the right, behind or in front.

Light from the **right,**
Light from the **left.**

Light from the **left,** but a low sun.

The **lower** the source of light, the longer the shadows.

The **stronger** the light, the darker the shadow.
The **softer** the light, the gentler the shadow.

Length of shadow

The shadows objects cast

Demonstration 6
Hatching and Crosshatching

So far we have looked at what I call traditional pencil shading, whereby altering the pressure on your pencil creates varying strengths of shading. There is another technique in which a variety of lines created by the pencil are used to create many other effects. I show below a selection of these marks. They come under four headings. HATCHING is the use of parallel lines. The closer together the pencil lines, the darker the area; the further apart, the lighter the area. CROSSHATCHING is where one set of hatching lines is placed over another set. STIPPLING is where dots are made with the pencil. The closer the dots are, the darker the area; the further apart, the lighter the area. RANDOM LINES are pencil marks, semicircles, ticks and wiggly pencil effects that do not fall under the other three headings, but can be very useful. Make out the chart below in your sketch book. Invent several more types of hatching, crosshatching and random lines of your own. The tree at the top right hand corner of this page shows how exciting and different the use of this technique can be.

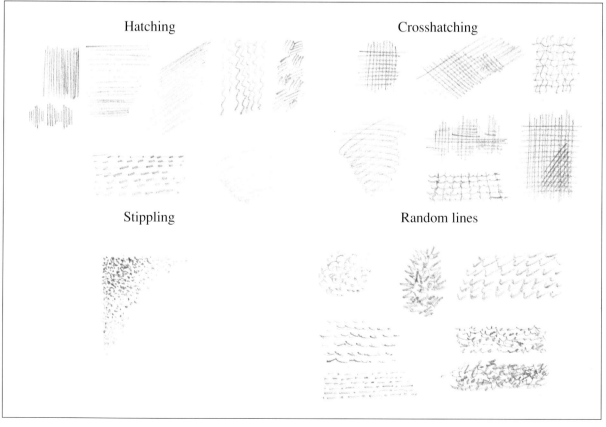

Hatching

Crosshatching

Stippling

Random lines

Demonstration 7
Textures: Tactile Values

A painting consists of three main parts: the sketch or drawing of the subject, the colouring in of it and the ability to show, or suggest, the material the subject is made from.

When you look at paintings by the great masters such as Rembrandt, Gainsborough or Renoir, you do not have to guess what the material was they were painting in any part of their picture. As artists, what we are trying to do is to trick the eyes of the onlooker into believing that a few marks of a pencil on paper, or paint on paper or canvas, is nothing of the sort, but is wood, silk, metal, hair, flesh, or whatever it is we are sketching. In fact, if you think of yourself as an illusionist you will be very close to understanding what much of sketching and painting is about.

We can use the traditional shading, hatching, crosshatching, stippling and random lines to gain an insight into the art of rendering textures, often referred to as tactile values. I would like you to find and sketch two quite different pieces of wood, one a piece of rough tree bark, the other a smoother piece. I show the types of wood below. With one I have used hatching and crosshatching to help convey the coarse, rough surface, and with the other I have used a softer, blended shading for the smoother effect. When you have tried this exercise, look around your home for a selection of subjects with a variety of different textures. A rubber glove, a broken brick, a milk bottle or glass and a child's furry toy are excellent examples. See if you can capture the textural effects of the subjects. When you show the resulting sketches to your friends or family, ask them what types of material they think the items are made from. If you are given the correct answer, well done. If they give a wrong answer, look at the surface of the object again and see if there is any more textural information you can add to your sketch. It is well worth trying two or three sketches each month of quite different textured items, to keep up the development of your skill in capturing textural effects.

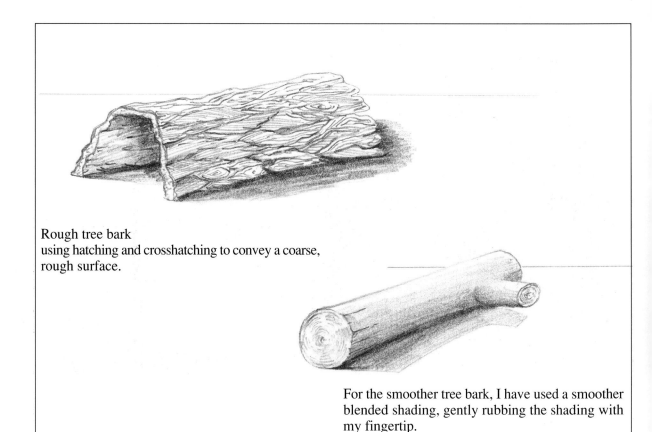

Rough tree bark
using hatching and crosshatching to convey a coarse, rough surface.

For the smoother tree bark, I have used a smoother blended shading, gently rubbing the shading with my fingertip.

Demonstration 8
Planning Your Picture: Still Life

Failing to plan is planning to fail. That is sound advice which applies to almost everything in life, and certainly to sketching and painting. Always choose subjects that you feel moved or inspired by. Never just paint a subject for the sake of it. It is always more enjoyable to paint inspirational subjects and this is often reflected in the quality of the work. Once you have chosen a subject, a little thought and planning goes a long way in helping ensure that you finish with a successful painting. Sketching plays a very important part in the picture planning stage. In the later stages of this book we look at picture composition, but I consider the making of preliminary sketches so important that I think this aspect should be considered at this stage. I will now take a still life subject and a lansdcape to illustrate the use, and advantages, of making preliminary sketches.

Preliminary Sketch 1 Top right.
I set up a simple still life subject on a table. I used a baking bowl, two eggs, a wooden spoon, a jug and a bag of flour. I wanted to be sure of the correct positions and proportions of the items in the still life in relation to the picture area on my sketch pad. Preliminary sketch number 1 gave me this opportunity.

Preliminary Sketch 2 Bottom right.
Here I looked for, and added, a little more definition to the objects, to give them more definite form.

Preliminary Sketch 3 Opposite.
In the third, far more completed sketch on the page opposite, I decided on the direction and strength of the light, located light, medium and dark tones, indentified the darkest features and highlights, and finally the position of the shadows. These three quite quick sketches helped me to really get to know the subject, to indentify and resolve any problem areas. At this stage I knew if I were to go ahead and use these preliminary sketches as the basis for a painting, it would be based on a sound foundation.

> HANDY HINT
> Let the first two preliminary sketches be the same size as your fininshed painting. Ideally the finished preliminary sketch should also be the same size, but if it is going to be a large painting then the finished preliminary sketch can be A4 or A3 size.

Preliminary Sketch 1

Preliminary Sketch 2

Preliminary Sketch 3

Demonstration 9
Landscape

With the landscape subject I used exactly the same sequence of steps as before, working from a simple preliminary sketch, below, to a more defined, light, outline sketch, top right on the page opposite, through to the shaded in, more defined sketch, below it. This approach may sound elementary to readers who are at an advanced stage in their painting, BUT it is a method I have used for over thirty years and it has never let me down. It is an excellent technique for people who are at the start of their sketching and painting activities and well worth more experienced painters trying out. Often the most successful of my students and course members are those who have adopted this approach. They find their paintings are based on sounder foundations than those who do not use it.

People often choose the first view of a subject they see, only to find that when they stop, stand up, and move from one side to another they find a more interesting, or unusual view, they wish they had worked from. If working from life, specially out of doors, it is well worth making several very quick sketches of your subject from different angles, to discover the best angle for the subject, even though you may end up coming back to work from the first view or angle you saw.

HANDY HINT

Most of the mistakes in a painting are made before the paintbrush is picked up. People are so keen to get on with the painting they quickly sketch out the picture, spend many hours painting on that sketch, only to find at the end any mistake in the sketch has been painted into the picture.

When you have made your sketch, BEFORE you shade it or paint it, STOP, turn the sketch upside down, or turn it to face a mirror and look at it in the mirror. Any mistake will show up and can be corrected. The corrections can be rechecked using the same methods.

Preliminary Sketch 1

24

Preliminary Sketch 2

Preliminary Sketch 3

Demonstration 10
Pen and Ink Sketching

We have looked at the use of a pencil for sketching, but there are many other items and materials which can be used by artists to create an extensive range of sketching techniques and to allow for the widest varieties of style and expression. Let us look at the use of pen and ink.

Pen and ink sketching is traditionally created using a bottle of black waterproof Indian ink and a dip-in pen. Most art shops and stationery stores keep mapping pens, or pen holders with separate pen nibs. Whilst nylon and felt-tip pens, technical drawing pens, biros and fountain pens can be used, so can sharpened matchsticks, cocktail sticks and sharpened bamboo.

PEN AND INK TECHNIQUE

Keep a spare piece of paper on the table by your side, so that as you dip into the bottle of ink you can test the pen stroke on the paper. This will ensure that there is not too much ink on the nib and that it won't blot. You may get one or two blots at first, but you soon come to know just how much ink to have on your pen. Keep a tissue in your non-painting hand so that every five minutes or so you can wipe your nib on it to stop the ink drying and clogging.

HATCHING is where parallel lines are used side by side in any direction. The closer the lines are together, the darker the area; the further apart they are, the lighter the area.

CROSSHATCHING is where the hatching lines are crossed over each other to achieve an effect.

STIPPLING is simply dots created with the tip of the pen. The more dots on an area, the darker it will become; the fewer dots, the lighter it will be.

RANDOM LINES are any type of line not covered in the other three groups. They could be tick-like marks suggesting tiles on a roof, or semicircles which could be used to create bushes and trees. On a piece of cartridge sketching paper practise the hatching, crosshatching, stippling and random lines I show in the panel on the right. When you have tried these, experiment and see how many other types of pen mark and effects you can achieve. Also practise varying the pressure you apply to the nib, the heavier the pressure, the thicker the line; the gentler the pressure, the finer the line.

Pen and ink is very similar to the work of engravers, who make marks with sharp tools on metal or wood, to create the plate from which their print is produced. The pictures on currency notes often incorporate extensive use of hatching, crosshatching and random lines shown in the right hand panel.

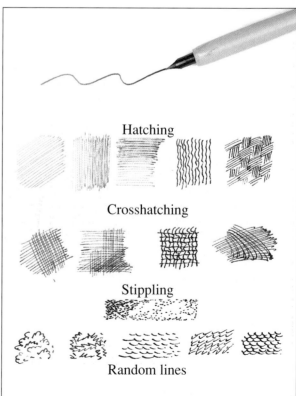

Hatching

Crosshatching

Stippling

Random lines

Experiment by drawing everyday items in pen and ink around your home and garden. Draw the outline of the items lightly first with a pencil, then overdraw with pen and ink. Try some items just using pen to outline them; the simplicity of this approach can be effective. Try sketching similar items using hatching and crosshatching to create the textures and shading. Use a putty eraser when the pen and ink sketch is dry, to lift out any pencil guidelines. With practice you will soon discover just the right amount of hatching and crosshatching to use. Look for other examples of pen and ink sketches you may find around your home, school or local library.

HANDY HINT
Stand your bottle of Indian ink in a clean, large, empty, plastic margarine or butter tub. If you happen to catch the bottle, and knock it over with your hand, this should help reduce any spillage or accidents.

A salt mill

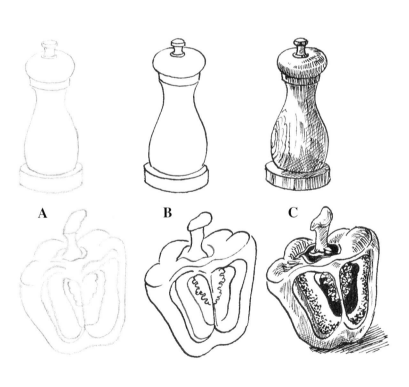

Look around the house and kitchen to find everyday objects to draw in pen and ink.

A. Sketch the object out in pencil.

B. Draw the outline in Indian ink with your pen.

C. Using hatching, crosshatching, stippling and random lines, add the shading and textural effects.

A red pepper cut in half

Demonstration 11
Roadside Houses

I sketched this view in the delightful village of Churchtown on the outskirts of Southport.

Stage 1. Sketch the subject in light outline using a 2B pencil on cartridge paper.

Stage 2. Lightly draw in the outline with pen and ink.

Stage 1

Stage 2

Stage 3. The light source is coming from the left, so the shadows are on the right of the objects in the sketch. The contrast between light and dark plays an important part in the success of the picture. Start using hatching and crosshatching to build up the shadows in each area. Use random lines to give the roof-tiles look, brickwork, foliage of the trees, texture of the foreground tree trunk, grass texture and windows in the way I show in the detail panel, below. If you try the pen and ink sketches in demonstrations 10 and 11, you should have an excellent start to understanding pen and ink sketching. Now go looking for more subjects of your own on which to practise this technique.

Stage 3

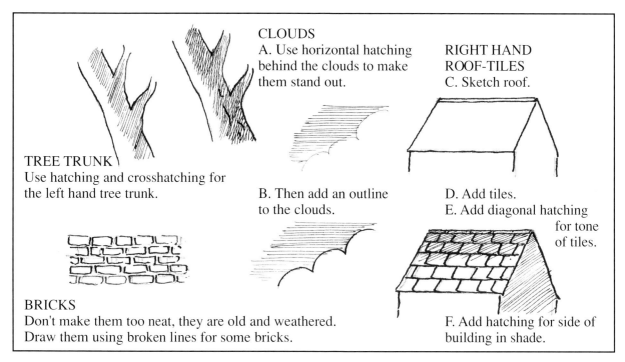

CLOUDS
A. Use horizontal hatching behind the clouds to make them stand out.

RIGHT HAND ROOF-TILES
C. Sketch roof.

TREE TRUNK
Use hatching and crosshatching for the left hand tree trunk.

B. Then add an outline to the clouds.

D. Add tiles.
E. Add diagonal hatching for tone of tiles.

BRICKS
Don't make them too neat, they are old and weathered. Draw them using broken lines for some bricks.

F. Add hatching for side of building in shade.

Detail

Demonstration 12
Stippling: Candle

In the panel on page 26 showing types of pen marks I illustrated an area with stippling. Stippling is done using the tip of the pen to create dots. This can be a fascinating way of creating pictures. In this demonstration I show a candle in a candle stick holder, which, when you have tried it out, might tempt you to try other subjects using the stippling technique.

Stage 1. Sketch the subject out lightly with your 2B pencil.

Stage 2. Using either your dip-in pen, or a medium or fine felt or nylon-tip pen, start from the top of the candle working your way down the picture stippling the whole subject. Use less dots in the lighter areas, increase them in the medium toned areas and add even more as each area, or part, becomes darker. Try to keep all the dots a similar size. Finally add the shadows of the background drape and tablecloth. Pastels, coloured pencils, coloured felt-tip pens, oil paint and acrylic paint can also be used for creating stippling paintings. The stippling technique was made very popular by the French artist, Georges Seurat.

Stage 1

Stage 2

Close up of stippling dots

Demonstration 13
Monochrome with Pen and Ink

The demonstration of the duck is an excellent way to recognise and understand the value of monochrome studies.

Stage 1. Draw the outline of the duck using a 2B pencil.

Stage 2. (Below) Make a tone strip using light, medium and dark areas of Indian ink diluted with water. Add more water to lighten the tones. You can check your brush strokes against the tone to be used.

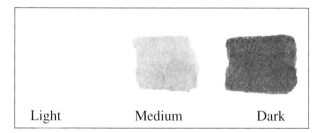

| Light | Medium | Dark |

Tonal Test Strip

Stage 3. Mix a light tone, brush that on the duck as shown. Let it dry. Leave white paper for the highlights.

Stage 4. Mix a medium tone and apply it as shown. Let the ink dry.

Stage 5. Mix a darker tone and apply it as shown. Let it dry.

Stage 6. Overdraw the pencil lines with pen and ink.

This demonstration helps you to understand about tone and the role it plays in sketching and painting. When you have tried the demonstration, look for subjects in colour and try sketching them using this monochrome technique.

I often make monochrome studies, either for my own enjoyment, or as advanced preliminary sketches for major paintings. I have selected three monochrome sketches painted over the recent years from my portfolio. These are shown on the next page.

Monochrome Studies From My Portfolio

Top right. I saw my mother's steam iron on the kitchen table and found the monochrome technique helped me resolve the tricky problems in sketching this subject. I took an oblique view from above, looking down onto the iron.

Bottom left. The Customs House, Kings Lynn. I made this monochrome sketch on location, and used it as a preliminary sketch towards making a finished painting of the subject.

Bottom right. There are subjects all around us. I once simply opened the bathroom door, sat on the landing floor, which gave me a lower eyelevel, and sketched our bathroom basin in monochrome. I used Indian ink diluted with water for the iron and Customs House. The bathroom basin was sketched using diluted writing ink. The iron and basin were overdrawn with felt-tip pen. The Customs House was overdrawn with pen and Indian ink.

Iron

Customs House, Kings Lynn

Bathroom Basin

Demonstration 14
Pen and Wash: with Water Colours - Cottage By The Sea

The previous demonstrations and advice provide a good foundation for all your future art work. Let me now introduce you to the joys of sketching with pen and wash in colour. A pocket set of water colours, a No. 6 or No. 8 round water colour brush, two pots of water, a water colour sketch pad, a 2B pencil, a putty eraser, together with your pen and ink, are all you need for this versatile technique.

Stage 1. Sketch out the subject with a 2B pencil.

Stage 2. Mix and apply a pale wash of colour for each area. Let it dry.

Stage 3. Mix and apply a medium tone wash for each area, leaving parts of the lighter tones showing through.

Stage 4. Mix a darker wash and apply it as shown in the Stage 3 picture. When dry, use a dip-in pen or a felt-tip pen and oversketch the picture. The resulting picture should have a sharp, crisp look to it. This technique can be used for producing quick sketches and finished art work.

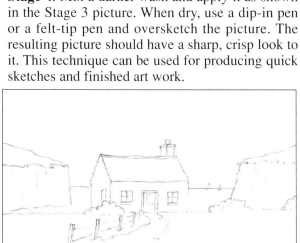

Stage 1

Stage 2

Stage 3

Stage 4

Santorini

SANTORINI · GREECE.

Philip Bevill 1987.

Notre Dame de Paris

A water colour painting, or an oil painting, may take several hours to paint, but a pen and wash sketch can be completed in a fraction of the time. It is for this reason I use the technique a great deal out-of-doors.

When I am out with family or friends, or travelling, I often see splendid and appealing subjects, but due to the very limited time available it is not possible to paint a finished picture. Pen and wash with water colour enables me to make a quick sketch, splash colour onto it, and overdraw the essentials with my pen and ink. I then not only have a presentable and attractive sketch in its own right, but a sketch that provides material which can be developed into a finished painting in my studio. Let me show you several situations where I used the technique quickly to produce pictures which have a freshness, or added quality, which may have been lost by having unlimited time available to paint them.

Santorini. Left.
I was tutoring on a cruise, sailing from Venice to Corfu, Dubrovnik, Santorini, through the Corinth Canal to Athens and on to Turkey. My task was to teach and demonstrate to the students on the cruise, not to go off painting my own pictures. But in free moments, coffee breaks and lunch breaks I would take out my pen and wash kit and sketch a view which caught my eye, like the breathtaking view in Santorini on the page opposite. The composition with the domed roof breaking the line of its distant hills was exciting. I had fifteen minutes to capture the scene. I used water colours on cartridge paper, overdrawing it with a fine felt-tip pen. Santorini, just for the price of a cup of coffee.

Notre Dame de Paris. Below.
Most people like to paint Notre Dame from the front. I was walking along the Left Bank in Paris, turned round and saw this rear view of Notre Dame. I knew I had to paint this view but it was soon going to rain. A water colour would have taken too long. The risk of rain made me select pen and wash. The sketch took thirty minutes. As I was packing away my materials the first rain drops started to fall.

Venice

Gondolas are as much a part of Venice as are the pigeons in St. Mark's Square. The joy of the city is that it has not had to be adapted to accommodate the motor car. Venice is a marriage of sea and land. Venice is liquid light, a place where the sounds and sights which have captivated artists, musicians and authors over the past centuries has also cast its magic spell over me.

Below. Become an explorer. On one visit to Venice I decided to visit an area of the city unknown to me. I came across the last gondola boatyard in Venice. I had my pen and wash kit with me. The sketch below took forty-five minutes using a felt-tip pen over a water colour sketch painted on 140lb "Not" water colour paper.

I was intrigued by the single large tree in the centre of the boatyard. This apparently has a design purpose; it is there to provide shade during the heat of the day for the boatyard workers. I was also intrigued to see the gondolas on their sides for repair... not quite the graceful upright position we see as they glide along the canals of the city.

Right. On another occasion I was teaching on one of my painting holiday courses in Venice. A particular view across the Grand Canal had often caught my eye and I felt it had the makings of a good subject. I liked the long, slender buildings and the Venetian lamppost. I discovered that if I sat on the pavement it would give me a low eyelevel and would have the effect of the lamppost appearing to intersect the line of the roofs. The top of the lamppost would be seen set against the sky. The lamppost also acted to link the foreground, the Grand Canal and the buildings on the other side of the canal. For speed I used pen and wash with water colour to capture one of my favourite views on paper.

> HANDY HINT. Pen and wash is addictive. Do not get hooked on it. The technique enables charming pictures to be produced so quickly that there is a temptation to draw black pen lines around every water colour painting to finish the picture quickly. Don't let pen and wash studies be more than 25% of your picture production. This way you will retain the enjoyment of the technique to the overall benefit of your painting.

Gondola Boatyard, Venice.

View across the Grand Canal, Venice.

Demonstration 15
Flowers: Daffodil

How fortunate we are to be surrounded by so much natural beauty. Throughout the seasons we have an ever-changing wealth of flowers in our gardens, parks and florists shops. We grow them for our enjoyment and send cut flowers and potted plants as gifts to relatives and friends on special occasions. Whilst floral painting deserves a whole book to itself, you can start to sketch flowers from the very first day you pick up a pencil and paper. I have shown several sketches which you may like to try. They are an excellent way to start floral subjects.

Daffodil.
This was a single bloom with leaves from our garden, cut and placed in a tall, thin, clear, glass vase of water. The vase had a heavy base. I allowed the flower to curve slightly to the right, rather than have everything too straight. Choose a similar subject from your garden or use this study. Sketch the subject out with a 2B pencil. Using water colours tint the flower, stem and leaves of the flower, leaving the vase in pencil. The idea of using just a splash of colour in a sketch, to focus attention on the main feature, can give a distinctive look.

Rose.
At first, choose flowers with distinctive petals and leaves, do not paint very small flowers. The rose is perhaps one of the most beautiful of flowers. I bought this single rose for my daughter but could not resist sketching it. From one rose you can produce four different types of sketch and learn so much about each technique and the structure of the flower. The top left study shows the rose just in pencil outline. The top right study is a pencil sketch with the addition of shading. The bottom left study is a water colour sketch. Finally try the sketch in water colour overdrawn with pen and ink. One subject, four different treatments. If you try four studies of a different flower each month, you will soon gain expertise in sketching and painting flowers.

Demonstration 16
Rose

Pencil outline

Pencil with shading

Water colour

Water colour overdrawn with pen and ink

Demonstration 17
Colour Notes

As we are now using water colours as an important part of adding colour to our sketches, you will find it helpful to make out the colour chart on the right. Whilst most water colour boxes have a good selection of colours in them, many colours can be made by mixing just three PRIMARY COLOURS, Red, Yellow and Blue. By mixing any two of the three primary colours, you make the SECONDARY COLOURS. Red and Yellow make Orange, Yellow and Blue make Green, Blue and Red make Mauve. If you mix any two of the secondary colours, you make the TERTIARY COLOURS. Orange and Mauve make Dark Brown, Orange and Green make Light Brown, and Mauve and Green make Olive Green. By mixing the three PRIMARY COLOURS, Red, Yellow and Blue, with very little water you can make Black. Brown and Blue mixed together will make Grey.

The water colour sketch shown below is of items that were lying on our kitchen table one morning, an eggcup, a spoon and a knife. This sketch was painted using colours made by mixing the three primary colours.

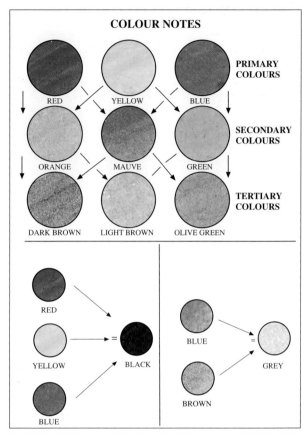

COLOUR NOTES

RED | YELLOW | BLUE — PRIMARY COLOURS
ORANGE | MAUVE | GREEN — SECONDARY COLOURS
DARK BROWN | LIGHT BROWN | OLIVE GREEN — TERTIARY COLOURS

RED + YELLOW + BLUE = BLACK

BLUE + BROWN = GREY

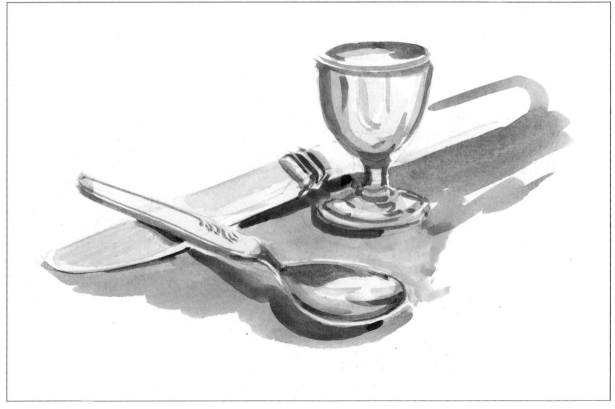

40

Demonstration 18
Pinocchio: Mixed Media

It is important to learn how different mediums can impart their own distinctive look to a subject. In this demonstration I used Pinocchio, a wooden doll I once bought for my daughter. He is a cheerful fellow and very colourful.

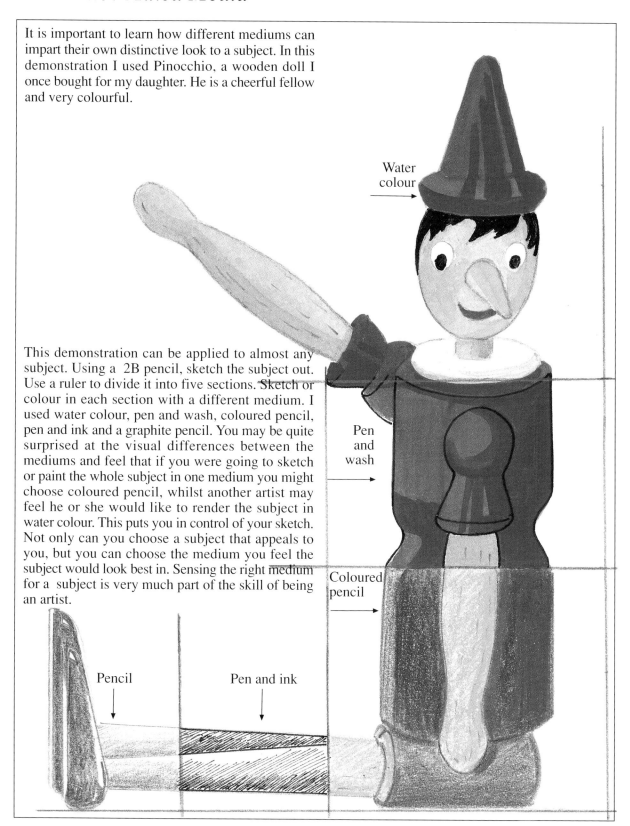

Water colour

Pen and wash

Coloured pencil

Pencil

Pen and ink

This demonstration can be applied to almost any subject. Using a 2B pencil, sketch the subject out. Use a ruler to divide it into five sections. Sketch or colour in each section with a different medium. I used water colour, pen and wash, coloured pencil, pen and ink and a graphite pencil. You may be quite surprised at the visual differences between the mediums and feel that if you were going to sketch or paint the whole subject in one medium you might choose coloured pencil, whilst another artist may feel he or she would like to render the subject in water colour. This puts you in control of your sketch. Not only can you choose a subject that appeals to you, but you can choose the medium you feel the subject would look best in. Sensing the right medium for a subject is very much part of the skill of being an artist.

Composition

The sketch or drawing of the subject you are going to paint, the skill in your colouring of it, the illusion of the textural effects, use of light and shade are all important elements of your painting. Another aspect equally important and which I come to now, is the composition of a painting.

There are certain guidelines, that if followed, can help you build your work on sound compositional foundations. One of the most important things is to avoid having any line or object that cuts your picture into two equal halves, as in view A below, where the horizon is on the halfway line and so divides the view into equal horizontal halves, and in view B, where the tree trunk divides the view into two vertical halves. Set any such line or object to one side or other, as in C and D. The horizon is just below halfway and the tree trunk to the left of halfway.

FOCAL POINTS AND KEY LINES (RIGHT)
Decide what it is that you want the people looking at your painting to look at in particular. The eyes should not be left to wander as if the viewer is lost. You are the artist, you are in control, be decisive.

A picture should have a FOCAL POINT, that is a main feature to which the eyes are led. I show three views. In E, the Focal Point, the barn, is in the middle distance, in F, the Focal Point , the castle, is in the far distance, and in G, the shed which is in the foreground is the Focal Point.
A picture should also have KEY LINES of the composition leading the eyes of the viewer to the FOCAL POINT. I have arrowed the key lines of the three compositions and I think from these illustrations you will see how the use of the Focal Point and Key Lines helps bring a composition together.

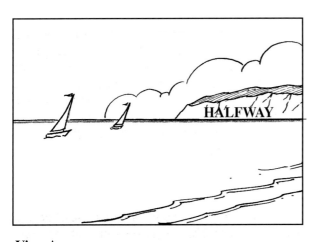

View A

View C

View B

View D

42

View E

View F

View G

THE TRIANGLE

A triangular shape often makes for a good picture composition. If you look at many of the paintings or prints that catch your eye and analyse them, they will have an underlying triangular structure to the composition.

I show three triangular compositions. In H, the still life, the table lamp and spectacles form the upright side of the triangle. In I, the tree to the right of the bridge helps form the apex of the triangle, which is just to the right of the centre of the picture. In J, the apex is on the right of the picture, and the sloping top edge of the triangle takes us to the building which is the focal point of the picture.

A good composition should have a sense of height, width and depth. The triangular shape is often helpful in ensuring this is achieved.

View H

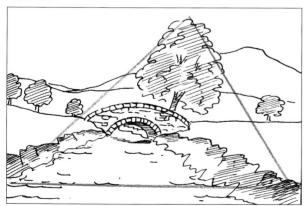

View I

View J

Perspective

Perspective is the one area of drawing and painting in which most people experience some degree of difficulty. When people hear perspective mentioned, they often go to a bookshop or a library, obtain a book on the subject, flip through it, see lines shooting about all over the place and usually end up more confused than before they opened the book. The secret is to keep the whole business of perspective as simple as possible, to remember a few basic rules, and to bear in mind that perspective is not something one masters in one, two or three lessons. Learning about perspective is an ongoing process. One goes along over a period of months, indeed years, collecting together the pieces of information, like pieces of a jigsaw, until they all fit together and the picture, the theory of perspective, becomes clear and easy to apply to one's work. Men used to have an advantage over the ladies when taking up

harmony and colour balance. I am pleased to say with the introduction of teaching technology to girls as well as boys at school, this should change in the future.

The eyelevel is an imaginary horizontal line across your field of vision when you look straight ahead: not up, nor down, but straight ahead. In my sketch I show a figure sitting low down, standing as if on a beach, then standing on a sand dune. Note how the eyelevel is always directly ahead of the figure. When looking at a real subject look straight ahead, hold a ruler straight out with the thin edge in front of, and across, your eyes that is where your eyelevel is. Which comes first, the drawing of the eyelevel or the subject? Generally I suggest you draw the object lightly first, then apply the eyelevel and use it with the rules of perspective to check and correct the object.

drawing and painting, because at school they have learned basic carpentry and even some metal work. Some boys were taught technical drawing and on leaving school and entering working life the types of books, manuals and journals they read had line drawings, plans, front elevations and side elevations of all sorts of subjects in them. It is this

One way to see perspective in action is to picture the view looking along railway lines. They appear to merge in the distance. The sleepers appear to become smaller and closer together. The point where the railway lines appear to merge is known as the "Vanishing Point", V.P. We know they do not merge in reality. I show this in my sketch. I also show the

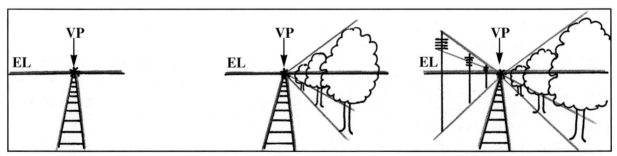

basic familiarity with line that proves very useful when learning to paint. Most ladies do not have that background experience, so I find ladies at first need more help with drawing. However, because of their knowledge from an early age of fashion, make-up and colour schemes, I find ladies are far more advanced than men in relation to colour, colour

railway lines with telegraph poles on the left, then with three trees on the right. The telegraph poles and the trees in a drawing or painting would also appear to become smaller and closer together as they recede. I have shown the guide lines for each item, illustrating how the guidelines all meet at the Vanishing Point, V.P.

Next I show a front view of a tool box. With this view there is just one vanishing point on the eyelevel for the sides of the box. I am imagining that I am sitting on a normal chair, at a table, when drawing the box in front of me. If I look straight ahead, over the box, my eyelevel line would be about 12" (30.5cm) above the top of the tool box. In my next sketch the box is set at an angle. We now have two vanishing points, one for each side. Guidelines will often want to converge at vanishing points off the page. This is quite normal and often happens. When it does, lay scrap paper at the side and tape it on from behind, then extend the guidelines onto it,

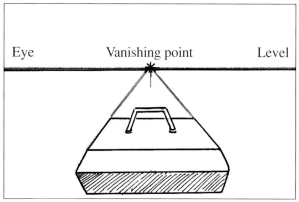

Tool box, front view

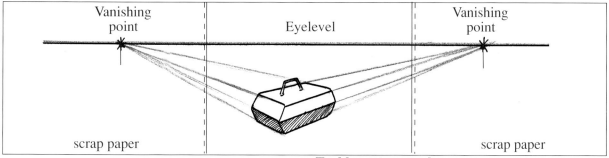

Tool box at an angle

in the way I show in my sketch. Never guess or assume the perspective is correct, always try to prove it.

Circular perspective.

Very few people realise that perspective can be used to help solve the problem of drawing circular and elliptical subjects, but it can. I have illustrated this with my sketch of two domestic paint cans and a paint roller. I have drawn the subject out and placed my eyelevel well above it. I have then drawn a light guiding square around each ellipse and have drawn those squares "in perspective", in the same way as the tool box. The squares for the ellipses each have their perspective vanishing points on the common eyelevel. Both the large can and the small can share the same vanishing point as those ellipses are on the same plane. The ellipses for the paint roller are set at an angle, on a different plane, and have a vanishing point on the eyelevel, but over to the left. Using the squares helps determine where each vanishing point should be, to ensure the true perspective of the subject when an ellipse is involved. I then go back to each square to check that the ellipse touches the centre of each side of the square it occupies, for provided it does, I know the ellipse must be in true perspective. The squares and guidelines can be gently rubbed out before you shade or paint your picture.

A church at an angle with 2 V.P.s

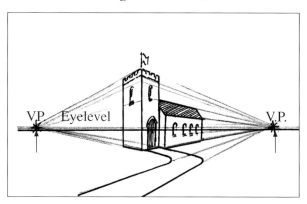

Circular perspective. Paint cans and roller

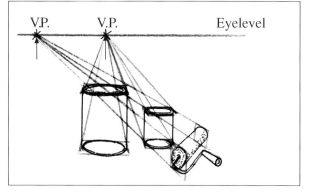

Demonstration 19
Faces

The following pages are intended as a guide. Almost all the headings on the pages that follow deserve an entire book to themselves. Faces are just an example. The important rule to remember is that THE HEAD IS AN EGG shape. If you remember this and use the halfway ellipses for proportions and for feature placement, along with my hints on sketching the features and practise the sketches I show, you should be able to sketch faces successfully.

Sketch A. The egg shape for the head.

Sketch B. Halfway lines. The centre of the eyes are on a line halfway between the top of the skull and bottom of the chin. The bottom of the nose is on a line halfway between the centre of the eye line and the bottom of the chin. The middle of the mouth is on a line halfway between the bottom of the nose and the chin. The top of the ears are just above the line for the centre of the eyes. The bottom of the ears are on the bottom of the nose line.

Sketch C. A line halfway across and straight down the centre of the face sees the eyes, nose, mouth and ears divided equally either side of it.

Sketch D. I have turned those halfway guidelines into ellipses and placed the features on them. This starts to bring the face into circular perspective and helps with any foreshortening of the face. We can now use head D and start to manoeuvre it to overcome all sorts of positional problems. Simply turn the egg and guidelines to the left, E, and to the right, F. Point the centre of the egg to the left or right and tilt it back, G. We can alter the incline of the head. To give the head backward look, H, place the curves steeper on the egg, or to give the downward look dip the curves downward as in sketch I. This helps achieve the foreshortening of the features and head. The contours of the face, hair and features can be built up on the foundation of the egg shape and guidelines of any face, J. Copy these sketches and then practise using photographs of faces and real faces.

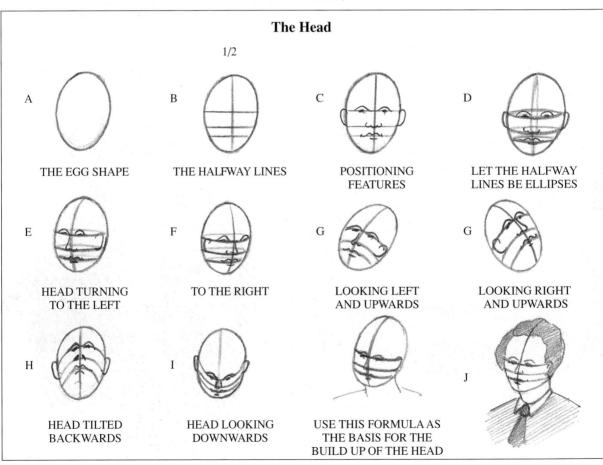

The Head

1/2

A — THE EGG SHAPE

B — THE HALFWAY LINES

C — POSITIONING FEATURES

D — LET THE HALFWAY LINES BE ELLIPSES

E — HEAD TURNING TO THE LEFT

F — TO THE RIGHT

G — LOOKING LEFT AND UPWARDS

G — LOOKING RIGHT AND UPWARDS

H — HEAD TILTED BACKWARDS

I — HEAD LOOKING DOWNWARDS

USE THIS FORMULA AS THE BASIS FOR THE BUILD UP OF THE HEAD

J

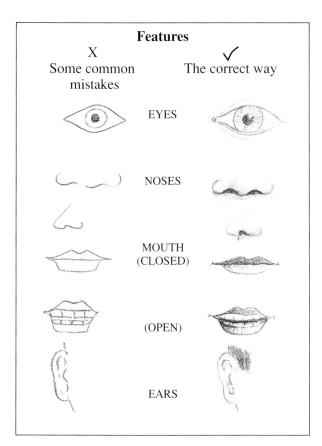

Features

X	✓
Some common mistakes	The correct way

EYES

NOSES

MOUTH (CLOSED)

(OPEN)

EARS

Practise sketching features from photographs and from life. Look in a mirror and sketch your own features. Avoid clumsily drawn features. Look at an eye and draw it. Note the tear duct in the corner near the nose, the highlight on the black pupil of the eye, the tone of the iris, the way the eyelids clip the top and bottom of the iris. Note the shading on the white of the eye and the shading in the folds of flesh above and below the eyelids. Note the shading under the lobes of the nose and nostril, and the shadow on the top lip.

When the mouth is closed the top lip is very dark. The lower lip has shading, but also highlights. Show the fine lines curving over the lower lip. When the mouth is open hint at the teeth and make the cavity in the mouth very dark. Avoid severe outlines.

The eyes, nose and mouth are dominant features. The ears are a secondary feature. Understate the ears; do not make them as clearly defined as the other features unless it is unavoidable.

Top left. Features
Bottom left. Girl, pencil sketch.
Bottom right. Man, felt-tip pen sketch.

Demonstration 20
Figures

Learning the proportions and developing a practical technique are the keys to sketching figures successfully. There are 8 heads in the length of the male figure, 7 1/2 heads in the length of the female figure and 4 1/2 heads in the young infant figure. Copy the proportion sketch on the right to imprint these proportions on your mind.

There are three types of figure in a sketch or painting, the far distant figure, the middle distance figure and the foreground figure. Let us look at proportions and techniques for sketching the middle distance figure as this is the type most often seen in general lansdcape sketches and paintings. The technique can be applied to all other figures.

Below. I show how to use match stick figures to position the figure. I add a chest and pelvis, locate the shoulder, elbow, knee joints, hands and feet. I usually sketch these very lightly in pencil and then sketch the actual figure and clothes on that foundation. The same technique can be used for standing, sitting, static or moving figures. Try pencil, pen and ink and biro sketches of these types of figures. Do not put in too much detail. Keep them simple.

The workman on the train, on the page opposite. This character was sitting just a few yards from me on a train one day. Using water colours oversketched with a felt-tip pen, I found the above figure drawing technique worked equally well for this closer figure.

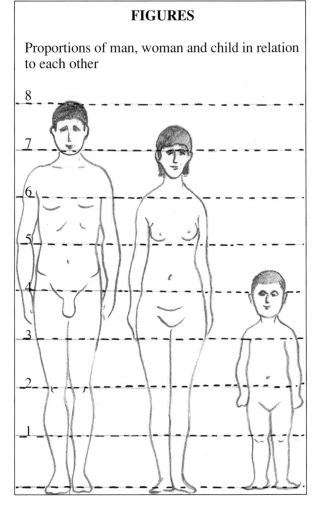

FIGURES

Proportions of man, woman and child in relation to each other

8

7

6

5

4

3

2

1

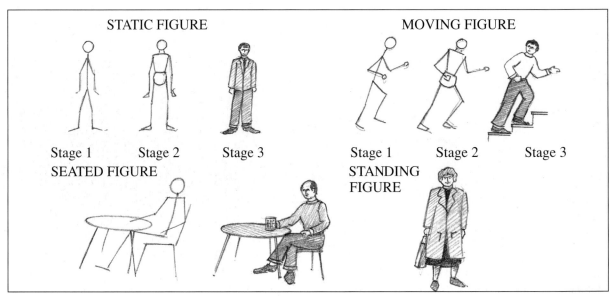

STATIC FIGURE

Stage 1   Stage 2   Stage 3

SEATED FIGURE

MOVING FIGURE

Stage 1   Stage 2   Stage 3

STANDING FIGURE

Workman on Train

Sketch of Manconian
Worker on train to
Southport. 15·7·70
P.E.J. BERRILL

Demonstrations 21 & 22
Sketching Out-of-Doors

Many people are apprehensive at first about sketching out-of-doors. There is no need to be. You can simply look out of your window and draw the view you see, or go into your back garden or a friend's garden and sketch a corner of it. There is nothing quite like sketching and painting out-of-doors. You become very much part of the scene which you are painting. When painting from a photograph everything you see has been frozen for a split second, but compare that to being out-of-doors, you can feel the warmth of the sun, the gentle breeze, the sky is active, the clouds move, the light changes, any water flows, you can hear the sounds of people, birds or other features which may be part of your subject.

A viewfinder, right, is a window 3" (75mm) x 2 1/4" (55mm) cut out of a piece of card 9" (230mm) x 6 1/4" (160mm). Held at arm's length this can be used to frame various areas of an outdoor view to help you decide what, and how much of the view, you want in your picture. Hold it horizontally, then see if you can find upright views by holding the viewfinder so the rectangle in the centre is vertical. Keep the subjects simple and not too cluttered.

If encountering tricky subjects like the rowing boat shown on the page opposite, use the basic shape idea as discussed on pages 15 and 16. Draw a box, find the centre of the top and front. Then draw the boat inside the box with the centre line to guide you for the position of the bow and stern.

Peel Harbour, Isle of Man, below. I was intrigued by the long, thin, horizontal picture possibility of this view. I drew a long, thin rectangle on my sketch pad and sketched the subject in pencil and water colour.

> **HANDY HINT.**
> When sketching out-of-doors keep the kit light and simple. An A5 sketch pad, 2B pencil, pencil sharpener, putty eraser, pocket set of water colours, a No. 6 or No. 8 round brush, small bottle of water, two small pots to pour the water into, some tissues to clean your brush and a fine felt-tip pen are all you need for many happy hours of outdoor sketching.

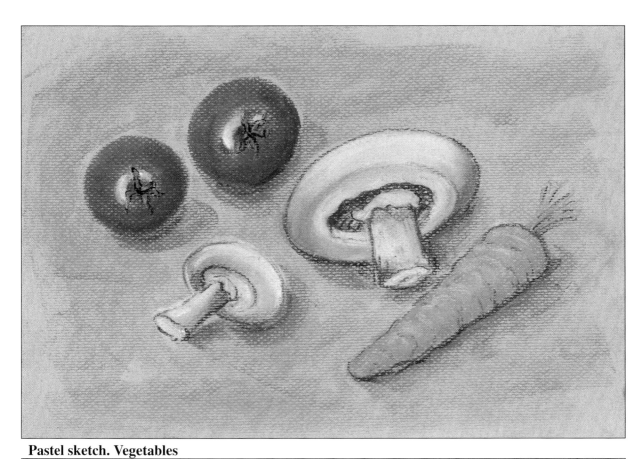

Pastel sketch. Vegetables

Pastel painting. Landscape

57

Demonstrations 27
Sketching with Oil Paints

Many artists paint with oil paints but do not realise you can use them for sketching. As oil paints normally require several days to become touch dry, many people think they are not a practical medium for sketching. I can tell you of two very successful ways to use them for this purpose.

Method One. The Tinted Canvas Panel. If sketching out-of-doors, take a canvas panel, your oil paints and materials with you, making sure you have some clean turpentine. When you find a subject that appeals to you, sketch it out lightly with a 2B pencil on the canvas panel. INSTEAD of using your oil paints thickly, as normal, do the opposite. Mix the paint thinly and tint the various coloured areas of the subject, or view, with a thin tint of its own natural colour. Within 30 to 60 minutes the turpentine will have evaporated and the panel will be dry. You can then take this panel, and others you may tint, home. On cold, wet, winter days, or dark evenings, take a panel out and paint the fully finished oil painting on top of your original, tinted, oil colour panel.

The same technique can be used indoors, but lends itself specially to outside painting expeditions and holidays.

Method Two. LIQUIN. Winsor and Newton produce Liquin, an alkyd resin, that you can mix with your oil paints instead of turpentine or linseed oil for normal oil painting techniques. It accelerates the drying of the oil paint. I use it frequently, and find if I am on holiday and mix Liquin with my oil paint to paint the oil paintings at the beginning of the holiday, the pictures are touch dry at the end of the holiday and can, with care, be transported home safely. Alkyd paints are synthetic paints similar to oils, but based in Liquin. They are normally touch dry within 18 hours.

HANDY HINT. Wear old clothes when working with oil paints. Oils are lovely to use, but dabs of colour can get on to your clothes, no matter how careful you are.

Subject. Lakeland bridge

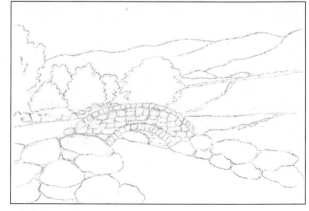

Subject drawn out on a canvas panel

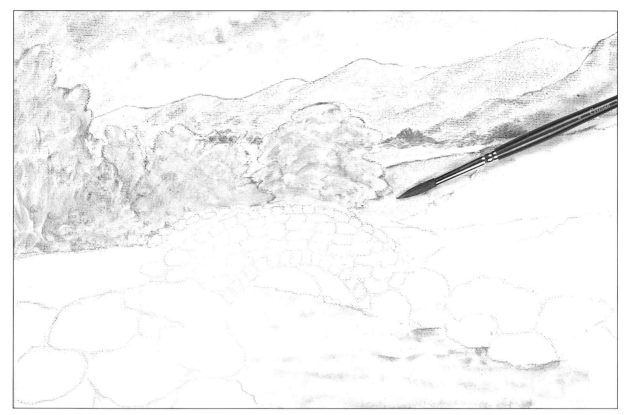

Part tinted Oil Panel Sketch

Finished tinted Oil Panel Sketch

Lord Street, Southport

Inspiration and imagination do not come in tubes or bottles. For twelve years I owned an art store and framed pictures. One day a lady asked to have a picture framed. Her husband was a keen fisherman and had been salmon fishing in Scotland. Whilst there he bought a long, thin, pencil sketch of the salmon river with inset sketches of the salmon pools along each side. It was a charming idea and the long, thin shape attracted me. Southport does not have a salmon river, but it has a very famous street over a mile long, called Lord Street. It is very straight and a central feature of the town with many historic buildings, shops and hotels situated either side of it. I thought I could adapt the salmon river idea to the

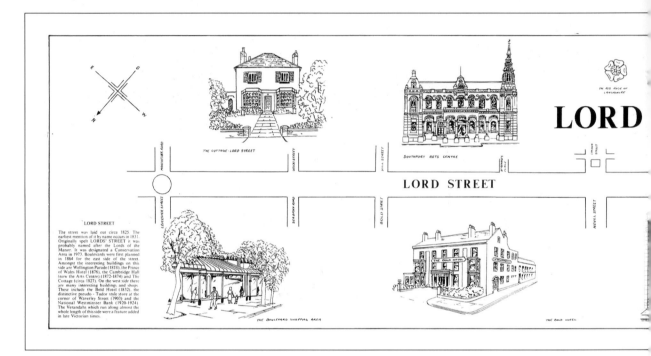

street featuring key buildings and the town's history instead of salmon pools. I selected the most interesting buildings, made sketches of them, and used pen and ink to draw out the finished art work in my studio. I had it screen printed. I sold it framed, and unframed, in black and white and hand water coloured versions. Measuring 91/4"(235mm)x36"(910mm) it has proved very popular with residents and visitors to the town. Southport's local authority commissioned 200 framed, slightly different versions of the print, to be the town's gift, presented by the Mayors of Southport to very important visitors.

Can you adapt a familiar location in an imaginative way?

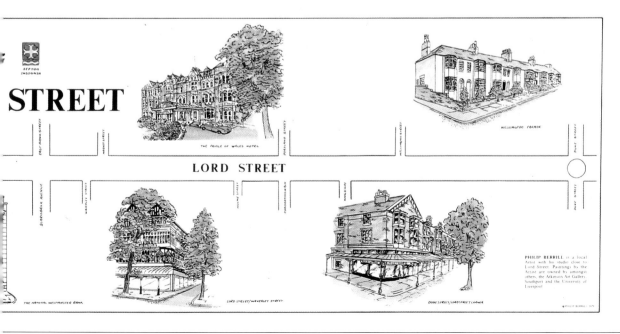

Framing Sketches

Keep loose sketches clean and flat in a portfolio. There will be sketches that you decide to frame and exhibit or sell. Some people make their own frames, but the majority of people call on the help of a professional picture framer, or buy and use many of the very good, ready-made frames and mounts which can often be found in art and framing stores. Some framers advertise a mail order service in art catalogues.

Pencil, coloured pencils, pen and ink, water colour and pastel sketches will need to be framed with a window mount of a suitable colour and under glass. The glass protects the picture from atmospheric soiling. The mount provides a border between the surrounding wall and the sketch and keeps the glass away from the immediate picture surface.

Oil paint sketches, which are not too thickly painted, can be framed the same way, but generally, and especially if thickly or robustly painted, oil paintings are varnished and framed without glass.

A good framer can be a very good friend, offering expert advice on what will show your sketches and paintings to the best advantage.

Sketch ready for framing

Picture mounts

Framed sketch

Exhibiting and Selling Work

Many people who take up the art of painting never think of the possibility of exhibiting or selling their work. Their first paintings are often given to family and friends, and people begin to see and admire their work. "How much do you want for that painting?" "Do you think you could paint me a picture of such and such?"

How do you price your pictures? How do you go about selling your work? The price you can command will depend on the type and quality of paintings and the state of the local economy. It would be nice to give a short answer on what to charge, but because of the above conditions I can't... but I can tell you people who can... your local framer, art gallery director, art club secretary or art school teachers. If you show them samples of your work, and ask them for honest pricing advice, they will usually be willing to advise you.

Art shops, galleries, hotels, furniture stores, department stores and gift shops often buy, or will display paintings for sale, taking a modest commission.

Your local library, art shop and art gallery will usually have details of forthcoming art exhibitions which you may be eligible to enter. There are lots of opportunities to exhibit and sell work... but above all else paint for your own pleasure and enjoyment. Exhibiting and selling work is a nice bonus when it happens.

Art clubs and art societies can be well worth joining. Libraries, art schools and newspapers will often be able to give you details of such groups. If you can't find a group...Why not start one yourself?

Below. Alan, Andrew and Sandra.
I discovered these young, talented teenage brothers and their sister painting superb pictures on Anglesey, North Wales. I was so impressed by the quality of their work I persuaded the art industry to sponsor their first exhibition at Holyhead. The exhibition, opened by the Mayor of the town, was featured on television.

SKETCHING

**Philip Berrill
"The Flying Artist"**

News Letter

is one of a series of art books which we hope you find helpful, enjoyable and informative.

The first four titles in the series are:

**Everyone's Guide to ... WATER COLOUR PAINTING
Everyone's Guide to ... OIL PAINTING
Everyone's Guide to ... PASTEL PAINTING
Everyone's Guide to ... SKETCHING**

These titles are available from bookshops and artshops or can be ordered direct from:
B.B.C.S.
P.O. Box 941
North Humberside
HU1 3YQ
England

If you would like to receive copies of Philip Berrill "The Flying Artist" Newsletters giving details of his demonstrations, talks, roadshows, painting holidays, videos and other interesting news, please write to:

PHILIP BERRILL "THE FLYING ARTIST"
PO Box 39, Southport
England PR9 9JA

Some helpful Do's and Don'ts

1. **Do keep a pocket sketch book and pencil by you at all times.**

2. **Do try to spend 10-15 minutes every day sketching something around your home or work place.**

3. **Do turn the sketch upside down, or look at it in a mirror to check for errors before shading or painting it.**

4. **Do experiment sketching with different mediums, pencil, pen, charcoal, pastel... anything that makes a mark.**

5. **Do go outside to sketch, as well as sketching indoors.**

6. **Don't forget to keep things simple, reduce things to basic shapes and build on the shapes.**

7. **Don't forget to take a camera with you if sketching out-of-doors; a sketch and a photo of the view can provide material for an original painting to be completed at home.**

8. **Don't forget to look after pencils, paper and your art materials. They will become faithful servants to your picture making.**

9. **Don't just sketch one view of a subject, try two or three sketches from different angles if possible.**

10. **Don't forget "ABS", Always Be Sketching.**